# THE AFFIRMATION
# OF IMMORTALITY

THE MACMILLAN COMPANY
NEW YORK · BOSTON · CHICAGO
DALLAS · ATLANTA · SAN FRANCISCO

MACMILLAN AND CO., LIMITED
LONDON · BOMBAY · CALCUTTA
MADRAS · MELBOURNE

THE MACMILLAN COMPANY
OF CANADA, LIMITED
TORONTO

# THE AFFIRMATION OF IMMORTALITY

*Being the Ingersoll Lecture
on the Immortality of
Man for 1946*

BY
JOHN HAYNES HOLMES

NEW YORK
THE MACMILLAN COMPANY
1947

# PREFACE

THE contents of this book were delivered as the annual Ingersoll Lecture at Harvard College on April 30th of this current year. This Lecture, given by a varied succession of men—scientists, philosophers, theologians, and ministers of religion—has sustained, through more than half a century, a continuous discussion of the great problem of death and life. If it has not solved this problem, it has clarified it, and brought conviction to many minds.

I am indebted to the College and to Dean Willard L. Sperry, of the Harvard Divinity School, for permission to publish the Lecture in this form.

1946                              J. H. H.

# THE INGERSOLL LECTURESHIP

*Extract from the will of Miss Caroline Haskell Ingersoll, who died in Keene, County of Cheshire, New Hampshire, Jan. 26, 1893*

*First.* In carrying out the wishes of my late beloved father, George Goldthwait Ingersoll, as declared by him in his last will and testament, I give and bequeath to Harvard University in Cambridge, Mass., where my late father was graduated, and which he always held in love and honor, the sum of Five thousand dollars ($5,000) as a fund for the establishment of a Lectureship on a plan somewhat similar to that of the Dudleian lecture, that is—one lecture to be delivered each year, on any convenient day between the last day of May and the first day of December, on this subject, "the Immortality of Man," said lecture not to form a part of the usual college course, nor to be delivered by any Professor or Tutor as part of his usual routine of instruction, though any such Professor or Tutor may be appointed to such service. The choice of said lecturer is not to be limited to any one religious denomination, nor to any one profession, but may be that of either clergyman or layman, the appointment to take place at least six months before the delivery of said lecture. The above sum to be safely invested and three fourths of the annual interest thereof to be paid to the lecturer for his services and the remaining fourth to be expended in the publishment and gratuitous distribution of the lecture, a copy of which is always to be furnished by the lecturer for such purpose. The same lecture to be named and known as "the Ingersoll lecture on the Immortality of Man."

# THE AFFIRMATION
# OF IMMORTALITY

# I

It was shortly after his conversion to Christianity that St. Augustine entered upon his life-task, which was to justify the Christian faith to an unbelieving world. Long a student of classical learning and a public teacher of rhetoric and argumentation, Augustine sought to establish the dogmas of the church on a basis of reason as well as of revelation. "I desired," he said, "to be as well-informed about metaphysical as about visible things, to be just as sure of them as I knew that 7 and 3 make 10."[1] Here was an attempt to subdue the affirmations of the soul to mathematical demonstration, and of course it could not be done. Though Augustine reared the most imposing structure of theological thought the world has ever seen, he fell far short of putting the articles of religious faith in the same category with scientific data. But it never occurred to him that failure to prove a spiritual speculation as surely as a mathematical proposition in any way invalidated the reality of things invisible. The "metaphysical," or theological, still stood, whatever the breakdown of substantive verification. In such case, it was the mind of man and not the truth of God which was at fault.

Today we are exactly reversing this operation. We are trying to prove reality by statistical tables, mathematical equations, geometrical theorems—by the formulae, in other words, of materialistic science. But when the invisible things of this world, the metaphysical or spiritual realities, are recalcitrant to this method of handling, we straightway declare them to be unreal, and therefore non-existent. We assume, in other words, that our processes of nat-

4

ural inquiry are quite adequate to all phenomena, our attempts to reduce everything to mathematical sign or physio-chemical symbol are infallible; and that any failure, therefore, on the part of the invisible to comply is proof positive that there is no reality to this invisible. Only what can be seen, and weighed, and measured, and standardized, is genuine. All else is shadow or superstition. So that the same discrepancy is used in our time to invalidate the "metaphysical" which, in St. Augustine's time, was taken simply to imply the incompetency of the finite human mind to make its way

> . . . through the Invisible
> Some letter of that After-life to spell.[2]

This outright repudiation of the idealistic, as Plato would call it, what Augustine himself termed the "metaphysical," betrays a dogmatism of which

5

the Bishop of Hippo would have been ashamed.

The low estate of the immortal hope today is due to the materialistic trends of this modern age, and more particularly to this refusal of a purely religious concept to fit itself into the framework of our physical methodology of thought. Insisting, as we do, that this framework bounds and thus encloses the entire area of reality, and finding the idea of immortality not definitely inside this framework, we promptly classify the doctrine as a fantasy of man's imagination, or a sheer wish-fulfilment in the forbidding face of death. In either case, it is not of interest to our contemporary thinking. In 1931, while in attendance upon this annual convocation, I talked with Professor Francis G. Peabody, and he asked me the subject of the Ingersoll Lecture to be given that day. "The subject," I said, "is 'Immortality and the

Present Mood.' " "Oh," said Peabody,
"it will be a short lecture, won't it?"
He understood that the modern mind,
using the sole language of materialistic
science, or mechanistic philosophy, is
contemptuous of the invisible which
uses a language of its own, and gives to
this invisible as short a shrift as most
of us give to the foreigner who insists
upon talking in his native German or
Russian tongue, instead of in our English. As though there were not as many
languages as there are phases of experience; and, as Moses discovered
when he was taught the name of God,
"I Am That I Am," an ultimate of
expression which is eternal being itself!
But the modernist wants a formula or
a statistical table. If there were only an
equation for immortality to match Ein-
stein's equation for relativity, then
we could believe the one as readily as
we believe the other, though both take

us into the realm of mystery. In the absence of such an equation, "the present mood" is negative.

## II

BUT WHY should we pay undue attention to this "present mood"—a mood which began with reluctant resignation, like that of Herbert Spencer in his last years, when he recorded in his *Autobiography* the "thought, so strange and so difficult to realize, that with death there lapses both the consciousness of existence and the consciousness of having existed,"[3] and has now reached the bumptious arrogance of H. L. Mencken, who lightly proclaims that he has "no desire for immortality" and that "the belief in it issues from the puerile egos of inferior men"?[4]

It is true that the modern mind has shown that we cannot prove that man is immortal. This conception simply does not lend itself to demonstration by naturalistic thinking. This is illustrated by the age-old desire of man to discover the reappearance of the dead, or to open up communication with them as still living. This effort is based upon the perfectly sound proposition that, if contact were established in only a single instance, this would be proof that there is another country beyond the grave to which some at least of the dead may voyage. So we try to see ghosts, to hear voices, to decipher writings, to touch ectoplasm, feeling that in such seeing, hearing, reading, or touching there will be first-hand experience of eternity. But always there is the baffling difficulty implicit in the fact that contact with the dead depends for its success upon some process of materialization, while immortality, by its very nature, must be a process of dematerialization. "For this corruptible must put on incorruption, and this mortal must put on immortality"![5] It is not inconceivable

that death may be able to reverse itself
—that the butterfly may be able to
make its way back into the cocoon. But
what I seem to see in this striving for
communication through the senses with
the dead is a rather pitiful endeavor to
identify spiritual reality with material
manifestation, which is an abandon-
ment of the whole significance of eternal life. Is this not the reason why, in
all the accumulated mass of testimony
on this point, much of it fantastic, most
of it dubious, a small part of it, as in
the case of the Betty Books,[6] deeply
impressive, there is nothing that is
really final? The very necessity of a
material medium to lead us into the
next world binds us inextricably to this
world, in the conviction set forth by
Maurice Maeterlinck in his *Our Eternity*, that, in seeking explanations of so-
called psychic phenomena, "we should
stay in our own world, [exhausting]

all the suppositions there to be discovered before leaving the terrestrial plane." [7]

Failing, therefore, any sure evidence of dematerialization, we have no proof, within the range of naturalistic thought, that man is immortal. But what of it? Where is the proof of other beliefs which we count as basic to the substance of our rational being, and never for a moment doubt at all? My personality, for example, my individual consciousness—what proof have I that I am I? How do I know that I am not fooling myself, like the lunatic who thinks he is Napoleon? Assuming that I am myself, as I do and must, how can I then be sure that my consciousness is awake? In a letter to a friend in 1923, Judge Oliver Wendell Holmes wrote: "I noticed once that you treated it as a joke when I asked how you knew that you weren't dreaming me. I was quite

12

serious. . . . We begin with an act of faith. . . . [For] you never can prove you are awake."[8] Then there is the perennial riddle of the freedom of the will, upon which rests the whole gigantic structure of the moral life. I seem to be free, no doubt about that—but how can I prove it? The materialist, or mechanist, can make a strong case against the postulate of freedom, and what can I say in answer?

The fact is that these ideas, and others like them which have to do with the soul and its functioning, are in no way susceptible of scientific demonstration. They yield to no syllogism, fit into no equation, cannot be measured, touched, or tested. We simply feel these things, that's all, as we feel a sunset, or a chord of music, or the love of an ideal, and find them real in our perception of experience. In his famous poem *Bishop Blougram's Apology*, Robert Browning raises the question of how unbelievers can be sure of maintaining their unbelief:

> . . . how can we guard our unbelief,
> Make it bear fruit to us?

That is "the problem here," he says. For

Just when we are safest, there's a sunset touch,
A fancy from a flower-bell, some one's death,
A chorus-ending from Euripides——
And that's enough for fifty hopes and fears,
As old and new at once as nature's self,
To rap and knock and enter in our soul.

This is what feeling does for us in making true what passes demonstration. Reality is what we feel and find within ourselves. Our personal identity, our moral freedom, our sense of beauty —these things are what we are, and therefore a part of being. And with them is the hope of immortality! Suddenly becomes crystal clear the great statement of James Martineau, "We do not believe immortality because we have proved it, but we forever try to prove it because we believe it." [9]

## III

IT IS obvious that there are two worlds in which we live, or rather two interpretations of the one world which is our home.

On the one hand is the physio-chemical world which is now attaining a kind of final triumph in the initial marvels and terrors of the atomic age. This world has to do with matter and energy, and the interaction, which has now become an identity, between the two. It deals with quantities and not qualities, with measurements and not values, with activity and not being, with phenomena and not noumena. It has nothing to do with such concepts as immortality, the reality of which it cannot even conceive, much less verify. A materialistic philosophy must remain absolutely neutral in the face of such a speculation as that of survival after death, for as it cannot prove, so also it cannot disprove, that man's life is eternal. In his little book *Life Everlasting*, John Fiske[10] discusses the argument that states of consciousness cannot exist apart from the activity of the material molecules that make up the substance of the brain. "How much does this famous argument amount to," he asks, "as against the belief that the soul survives the body?" And he answers, "Nothing! Absolutely nothing. It not only fails to disprove the validity of the belief, but it does not raise even a *prima facie* presumption against it." For our sensory experience in a material world cannot reach beyond itself. It is finite and not infinite in range, and therefore limited to its own areas of space and time—while "in all probability," continues Fiske, "there are immense regions of existence in every way as real as the regions we know, yet concerning which we cannot form the faintest rudiments of a conception. . . . The reason is obvious. . . . So long as our knowledge is restricted by the conditions of this terrestrial life, we are not in a position to make negative assertions as to regions of existence outside these conditions. We may feel quite free, therefore, to give due weight to any considerations which make it probable that consciousness survives the wreck of the material body."

This brings us to the second interpretation which man has imposed upon his world—namely, the spiritual. For man has not been content to live merely a "terrestrial life," or to restrict his interest and knowledge to the conditions of this life. Matter and energy have never seemed to exhaust for him the fullness of existence. On the contrary, man has found, as we still find today, that the most important experiences which we undergo are not explained by the interplay of matter and force; nor have we been willing to dismiss these experiences as fantasies, or superstitions, just because they defy the methods of the laboratory. All on the one hand that is basic, and all on the other hand that is beautiful and meaningful, we have found within ourselves as an immediate consciousness of reality. And this consciousness of our own we find abundantly confirmed in the consciousness of multitudes of men, among whom are some of the most exalted and profound thinkers who have ever lived. We call these thinkers, who have thus made direct contact with reality, and have reported it as a scientist reports his observations, or an explorer his discoveries, the mystics. And I have never been able to understand why the testimony of these mystics has not been generally accepted as a valid part of knowledge! Of course, our rationalistic age is all against it. This testimony cannot be verified by an objective criterion of truth. But here it is, a constant experience of the ages, verifiable if not by outward experimentation then by inward correspondence with itself. These seers have most of them been isolated from one another, have dwelt in far-flung lands and used alien tongues, yet in an unbroken succession, from Lao-tse to Emerson, they have borne a single witness to a single truth. Their reports, as Aldous Huxley has recently reminded us, constitute a "perennial philosophy"[11] which presents and interprets a reality not otherwise apprehended. It is on the basis of this philosophy that we affirm the existence in the cosmos, and in the heart of man, of a fundamental being which is spirit. In the cosmos, this being is known as God;

in the heart of man, it is known as the
soul; in relations between men, it is
known as conscience. From the standpoint of its operations, the spirit is a
form of power which amplifies, ele-
vates, and at last transcends that physical power which is active in the world
of natural phenomena. It is God at
work in the soul, and the soul in God,
in obedience to the moral law. From
the standpoint of its own inner being,
the spirit is at once the source and ful-
filment of all life, the secret of all value,
the means to the attainment of all ends.
It is God made manifest in time and
place for the doing of his infinite and
eternal will.

Now, the idea of immortality is part
and parcel of this "perennial philosophy" of the spirit. It belongs with
God, the soul, and conscience, as integral phases of reality. If we are materialistic, or mechanistic in our thought,

then there is no reason why we should believe in immortality, and many reasons why we should not. If as honest as Thomas H. Huxley, we will say, even by the grave of our beloved, as he by the grave of his dear son, "I neither deny nor affirm the immortality of man."[12] We stand neutral! But if we accept the spiritual interpretation of life, then we must likewise accept the conception of man's survival after death. To reject it, or even to doubt it, would be to cut one link in the chain which binds the whole together. It would be to falter and fail in following through the rigorous logic of our own thought.

It is to the greater glory of Plato that he made this plain in his philosophy. This philosophy is the clearest, as it is still the noblest, of the spiritual speculations of man. Plato's majestic conception of the realm of Ideas as the abode

22

of the eternal, his interpretation of earthly phenomena as so many shadows, or reflections, of these Ideas, his description of learning as "a recollection of ideas which we possessed in a previous state" of being,[13] all these are expressions of a thought which has illumined the ages and radiates splendor in our time. And along with these conceptions goes the belief in immortality. Plato's system of thought simply could not have held together without this projection of faith into the unknown. A future existence of the soul was as necessary to its integrity as a previous existence of the soul. The arguments which Plato offered for immortality are no longer impressive. The doubts expressed by Simmias and Cebes in the *Phaedo* were never satisfactorily answered by Plato's mouthpiece, Socrates. The thesis presented in the *Phaedrus* that "the soul through all her

23

being is immortal, for that which is ever in motion is immortal; but that which moves another and is moved by another, in ceasing to move ceases also to live. Only the self-moving, never leaving itself, never ceases to move, and is the fountain and beginning of motion to all that moves beside"[14]—the argument, in other words, from self-motion —this has today its fantastic aspects. But it leads to better arguments, couched in the language of our time, which sustain the fundamental proposition, established forever by Plato, that the immortal life is a necessary element in any spiritual interpretation of reality.

# IV

WHAT ARE these arguments which spring from the spiritual philosophy of a modern mind?

They begin with man. How are we to explain man apart from the hypothesis of immortality?

It is easy to explain the animal, and the animal part of man's nature, for these have to do with mere physical facts in the immediacy of experience. The animal is primarily concerned with the impression of the moment —sights, sounds, smells, as so many guides to the satisfaction of appetite. It is the instant sense of these impressions which constitutes life for the brute creation, not their coördination and direction, least of all their sublimation. One cannot imagine an animal, maimed in the senses of the body, developing, as Helen Keller developed, a full-rounded and continuing personality. But a human being has attributes which are his own, and which transcend the physical. He remains an animal, but only as the Fifth Symphony, played by a great orchestra, remains still a series of notes printed on sheets of paper. What is important to man is what is distinctive of him, as well called by Shakespeare "the paragon of animals."

Central to human nature, as contrasted with mere animal nature, is self-consciousness, the sense of personal identity, the Ego as an individuality set apart in its own right from all other individualities and from the world. It is this "I," myself, which not only feels sensations, but objectifies, surveys, and classifies them. The child does not begin life with this self-consciousness—the child is pure animal at birth! The Ego

26

develops and at last is born, as the
foetus is delivered from the mother's
womb, the former being the spiritual,
as the latter the physical birth. Tenny-
son has beautifully and precisely stated
it in his *In Memoriam:*[15]

> The baby new to earth and sky,
>     What time his tender palm is prest
>     Against the circle of the breast,
> Has never thought that "this is I":
>
> But as he grows he gathers much,
>     And learns the use of "I" and "me,"
>     And finds "I am not what I see,
> And other than the things I touch."

It is thus, says the poet, that the infant
rounds himself "to a separate mind,"
and becomes thereby a person.

The second distinctive attribute of
man is time—the sense of moments
passing one after another in a continuous succession. Time flows, like a river
—but the self-conscious individual re-

27

mains fixed like the landscape through which the river flows. In the early life of the human, as in the entire life of the animal, the point of central excitement is the present—what is happening at this immediate instant. And so it remains with most personalities, who are hardly more than children, to the end. But the Ego, *mirabile dictu*, is not confined to the now—not with persons who are mature! On the one hand, it can reach back, in memory, to experiences which have gone by, and thus constitute the past; on the other hand, it can reach forward, in anticipation, to experiences which have still to come, and thus constitute the future. A self-conscious personality, in other words, is not confined to the present, but moves easily and freely in the past and in the future. As life ripens and experience deepens, the past, to a person of the meditative type, becomes more im-

28

portant than the present; and, to a person of the prophetic type, the future more momentous than either. But the great thing is that past, present and future are recognized as integral parts of the stream of time. "In rivers," wrote Leonardo da Vinci, "the water you touch is the last of what has passed and the first of that which comes: so with time present."[16]

But time, thus interpreted, becomes eternity, which is the third distinctive attribute of man. The stream of time is a single stream, as the waters of a river are an unbroken flow. Past, present and future, in other words, are no sooner seen distinct and apart than they are suddenly absorbed into a continuum which never begins and of course can never end. "Time," says Henry David Thoreau in *Walden*, "is but a stream I go a-fishing in. I drink at it; but while I drink, I see the sandy bottom and detect how shallow it is. Its thin current slips by, and eternity remains."[17] Remains for man to discover and apprehend as the supreme experience of his life—this eternity of which time, with its measured hours and years, is the mere appearance! But how discover and apprehend, if not by an innate sympathy of nature? Eternity is not a sensation to be felt, but a condition to be known. It is a reality to be lived in, as the mystics have lived in it with an intensity of realization surpassing all fleshly experience. If man is thus immediately conscious of the eternal, it must be because he is himself eternal. He recognizes without what he already knows within. Like Thoreau, gazing into the "thin current" of the running stream,

> Our souls have sight of that immortal sea
> Which brought us hither.[18]

30

In his great novel *Far From the Madding Crowd*, Thomas Hardy pictures a clear night when "the twinkling of all the stars seemed to be but throbs of one body, timed by a common pulse. . . . To persons standing alone on a hill during a clear midnight such as this," writes Hardy, "the roll of the world eastward is almost a palpable movement. . . . The poetry of motion is a phrase much in use, and to enjoy the epic form of that gratification, it is necessary to stand on a hill at a small hour of the night, and . . . long and quietly watch your stately progress through the stars. After such a nocturnal reconnoitre, it is hard to get back to earth; and to believe that the consciousness of such majestic speed is derived from a tiny human frame."[19]

But this "consciousness" is not "derived from a tiny human frame"! That is just the point! If man were no more

31

than such a "frame," then he would see no more of reality than the animal sees, and feel no more of reality than the animal feels. But as it is, man sees "the twinkling of all the stars" and "the roll of the world" through space, and feels the "common pulse" which throbs through the "one body" of the cosmos. Which means that man sees not merely with the physical eye but with "the mind's eye, Horatio," and feels not merely with the flesh but with the spirit! For man is spirit, as the universe is spirit. "Spirit with spirit can meet"— as spirit does meet with spirit in the self-consciousness of a personality moving through time into eternity. When man discovers the eternal, he discovers his immortal soul, and its abiding life in God.[20]

There are various ways of stating this argument from a less metaphysical and more practical point of view. One such way I first encountered, years ago, in James Martineau's *A Study of Religion*, and it made an impression upon my mind which has endured to this hour. As a mere animal, a creature of time and not of eternity, man is ridiculously, unaccountably overendowed. "The outfit of the animal," writes Martineau, "seems an ideal provision for the purely terrestrial sphere in which he is placed, while the outfit of man, if the terrestrial sphere be all that is appointed for him, seems clearly a vast over-provision."[21] If this life be all, in other words, what use has man for all these extraordinary mental and moral powers which distinguish him from the animal? Why should he not prefer, if survival upon this earthly planet be the only question, the swiftness of the deer, the strength of the lion, the vision of the eagle? What we have here is a fundamental lack of adjustment between

33

the endowment of man and his temporal habitat, which argues an unparalleled violation of the economy of the universe. There is a vast disproportion, in other words, between the constitution of the human mind and the demands of a purely transient existence. "Some sort of proportion we expect," says Martineau, "and never fail to find, between the endowment of a nature and the persistence and range of its achievement; just as, in human productions, the material selected and the refined pains spent in perfecting them are no uncertain index of the service expected from them. . . . For a week's encampment, you spread your canvas and do not build of stone. . . ." For a short voyage down the coast, you do not lade your vessel with store and cargo for distant seas. "When, on this principle," continues Martineau, "you place side by side the needs of human

34

life . . . and the scope of the intellectual powers of man, I shall be surprised if you do not find the latter to be an enormous over-provision for the former." And why such an over-provision except on the supposition that man is being equipped here for another and a vaster life?

But the really dramatic disproportion is not so much between man's mind and its environment as between man's mind and his body. If these two elements are to be regarded as aspects of a single integrated life, adapted to the conditions merely of this passing earthly existence, why do they pull apart instead of pulling together, and the weakness of the latter so often frustrate and defeat the former? What are we to think, for example, when a great and potent personality is suddenly cut off by an automobile accident, a disease germ, or a bit of poisoned food? Must

35

it not be what George Herbert Palmer thought as he looked upon the dead body of his wife, one of the outstanding women of her time—"Though no regrets are proper for the manner of her death, who can contemplate the fact of it, and not call the world irrational if out of deference to a few particles of disordered matter, it excludes so fair a spirit?"[22]

More serious is the discrepancy between mind and body in the waxing years of age when the spirit burns to an ever brighter flame, as the flesh crumbles slowly away to ashes. It is argued that the mind wanes as the body wanes —that the two are synchronized in a way to indicate the utter dependence of the former upon the latter. But this is not true! Last September there died a distinguished musical composer, Béla Bartok. In the last weeks of his life, he was engaged in the composition of his

36

third concerto for piano and orchestra. In his last hours, he worked feverishly to finish the piece, and succeeded with the exception of the last seventeen bars of the last movement. The concerto was a masterpiece, for, says a scholarly commentator, "though the composer was seriously ill, the vigor of his intellect was undiminished."[23] This experience is common and not rare. Victor Hugo was only one of many aging veterans who cried out against the limitations of the flesh, protesting that they had said and done not a thousandth part of what was in them. Such experience, oft repeated, prompts the sober philosophical statement of Professor William Ernest Hocking, that "to cease at the point of any attainment is to lose the full meaning of that attainment. From the mere logic of meaning, then, there is no moment at which conscious existence could appropriately cease."[24]

But it is the poets, as always, who state the final truth. Thus, Robert Browning, in his poem *Cleon*, makes his hero say:

. . . Every day my sense of joy
Grows more acute, my soul (intensified
By power and insight) more enlarged, more
    keen;
While every day my hairs fall more and more,
My hand shakes, and the heavy years increase
The horror quickening still from year to year,
The consummation coming past escape,
When I shall know most, and yet least enjoy.

The dying body and the quickening mind! How meet the challenge of this discrepant fact if not by doing what Cleon did, what men have always done——

    . . . imagine to [our] need
    Some future state.

Such imagination to our need takes on peculiar pertinency in relation to the values of man's life as his own achievement. "It is man," says the sage Confucius, "that makes truth great, not truth that makes man great." [25] Consider the world with man eliminated from the scene! The sun would be here, and the stars. Mountains would still lift themselves to the skies, and oceans roll to vast horizons. Birds would sing, and leaves rustle, and sunsets glow. But all this would mean nothing without man to see and interpret. What do the stars mean to the eagle, or the sea to the porpoise, or the mountain to the goat? What these things are in beauty, man has made. It is his ear which has heard the cuckoo as "a wandering voice," his eye which has seen "the floor of heaven thick inlaid with patines of bright gold," his mind which has found "sermons in stones, books in the running brooks, and good in everything." In Washington Irving's charming essay on "Abbotsford," which recounts his experiences as a young man in visiting Scotland and the home of Sir Walter Scott, he tells of going to Ayr, to see the birthplace of Robert Burns. He encountered there an old carpenter who had known Burns, and who took delight in showing the American author the beauties of Ayrshire, all made so familiar by the poet's songs. And Irving quotes the Scotsman as saying that "it seemed to him as if the country had grown more beautiful since Burns had written his bonnie little songs about it."[26]

It is thus that man creates the values of his world, or rather discovers these values as they were created of God. What man does with the world, in painting, poetry and music, is the soul's disclosure of reality. Yet it is suggested that the soul which sees and glorifies the whole shall perish while the world lives on. Such suggestion is irrational.

In the case of man as of God, the being who creates the world must himself be greater than the world. The spirit which conceives Truth, Goodness and Beauty must itself be as eternal as the Truth, Goodness, and Beauty which it conceives. Nothing has value without man. Man, therefore, is the supreme value. And value is what endures.

It is this logic of value which brings us to immortality as a concept of thought. This being so "noble in reason," so "infinite in faculty . . . in form and moving how express and admirable, in action how like an angel, in apprehension how like a god, the beauty of the world, the paragon of animals" [27]—how can this being perish like an animal? On occasion, to be sure, he seems to perish unnaturally and thus more terribly than an animal. Thus, in some great crisis, he refuses to bide his time, or wait upon accident, but deliberately stakes his life upon some "hazard of new fortunes," or sacrifices it for some heroic cause. If he lives out the Psalmist's span of years, in other words, it is not in mere adaptation to things of earth. On the contrary, almost from the beginning, he seems to strive to reach out, and climb up, and look beyond. There stirs within him something not of this earth, which teaches him to shun, even to despise in his best moments, the trammels of dust and flesh. Which means, or would seem to mean, that man exists for something beyond this present world! Living under the impulse of forces and to the pursuit of ends which have no permanent, or even natural, relation to this present realm of time and space, he must be destined to some farther realm where these forces and ends may find a resolution, as in a chord of music, which completes the stress and strain of long-

42

sustained disharmonies. What this farther realm may be, we do not know—even that it is a realm, and not some purely ideal state! But that its essence is a concept of immortality which matches the exactions of human nature would seem to be a corollary of reason.

## V

As THE immortal hope, interpreted as an aspect of spirituality, thus fits human nature, so also does it fit the universe. It is an answer to the challenge of outward as well as of inward realities of being.

In his earliest period of thought, man seemed to find purpose in the universe. Long before he had evidence to substantiate his belief, he formulated the idea that the world existed for some end. It was not a mere merry-go-round, turning and turning upon itself till motion ceases. It was not a mere game, like Omar Khayyam's game of cosmic chess, in which "the Master of the Show" takes men as pawns

Upon this Chequer-board of Nights and Days,
    Hither and thither moves, and checks, and
      slays,
And one by one back in the Closet lays.

It was not a play, or revel—an "unsubstantial pageant," in the words of Shakespeare's Prospero, which at the close leaves "not a rack behind," and men as

> . . . such stuff
> As dreams are made on; and our little life
> Is rounded with a sleep.[28]

Least of all was it to be regarded as

> . . . a tale
> Told by an idiot, full of sound and fury
> Signifying nothing.[29]

Life had meaning, significance, end and aim, design and purpose. It had a motive, like a piece of music; it was a process, like a growing flower. In this vast array of earthly phenomena, there was an idea being unfolded, a work being wrought. What man saw in the universe was a power which knew what it was doing, and why.

If evidence for this thought was lacking, as in the case of Aristotle, it was offered in abundance at the hands of Darwin. No one who did not live through it can imagine the excitement occasioned in the last century by the doctrine of evolution, and the contribution it made to the philosophy of purpose. What had formerly been a speculation was now become a record. Here in fossil rocks, in petrified bones, in vestigial forms of organic growth, were marked the progressive stages of life's development. From lower to higher creatures, from unicellular to multicellular organisms, from vegetable to animal, from invertebrate to vertebrate, from the fish and the bird to the mammal and the primate, always from the simple to the more complex and the more intelligent, so the line ran; until at last, after thousands of centuries, man appeared upon the scene as the

crown and climax of the whole. And
what is man? According to the physio-
chemical scientist, nothing but one
more step in an automatically unfolding process. Ernst Haeckel, one of the
three great evolutionists of his time,
identified to his own satisfaction no less
than twenty-six stages in man's development from an original chunk of car-
bon, and at no one of these stages found
anything beyond a recurrence of mere
mechanism. But others have found a
deeper and truer significance in man—
a goal reached, a design fulfilled. For
man is Nature's escape from mechanism—a spirit free for good, and alas, as
we see so tragically today, for evil.

In this evolutionary process, we see
the unfolding of what has been implicit
from the beginning. Man has not just
happened in the cosmos, any more than
*Hamlet* just happened in the brain of
Shakespeare. There is consciousness at

47

work here, and consciousness moved by purpose to some end. And this end must be Spirit, else there is no end to justify the intricate and costly process of creation which has been going on through eternities unknown. For sooner or later this material universe is going to dissolve and disappear. In the words of Robert Frost:

> Some say the world will end in fire,
> Some say in ice . . .[30]

Either element "would suffice," says the poet. Just how or when this last day is coming, no one can tell. There are scientists who contend that the universe is running down, like a clock, and thus at last must lapse into one dead level of inanition. Others assert that the universe is all the time winding itself up, and thus must finish in some cosmic cataclysm which will restore primeval chaos. In our own time we face suddenly the prospect of a final explosion of atomic energy, set off by our own degenerate hands, to rend the planet and leave a darkened void in the skies. In any case, there will come an end to all things earthly. Over the whole process of the æons gone will be scrawled the epitaph, "Vanity of vanities; all is vanity." That is, if there be no purpose in the process! If the evolution of material phenomena contains no aim beyond itself! Only if something survives out of the process to carry on, can its labors be explained and justified. And what can that something be but man who defies the crash of worlds? Man who lives on because he is in essence spirit—and spirit is eternal!

It is this argument which opened the agnostic mind of Charles Darwin to conviction on immortality. With respect to this question, he wrote, "Nothing shows me so clearly how strong and

almost instinctive a belief it is, as the
consideration of the view now held by
most physicists, namely, that the sun
with all the planets will in time grow
too cold for life. . . . Believing as I
do that man in the distant future will
be a far more perfect creature than he
now is, it is an intolerable thought that
he and all other sentient beings are
doomed to complete annihilation after
such long-continued slow process. To
those who fully admit the immortality
of the human soul, the destruction of
our world will not appear so dread-
ful." [31] In the light of the impending
"destruction of our world" at this moment, what else can serve to sustain us
at all? John Fiske saw the truth, with
a religious passion denied to Darwin,
when he wrote, "The more thoroughly
we comprehend that process of evolution by which things have come to be
what they are, the more we are likely

to feel that to deny the everlasting persistence of the spiritual element in man is to rob the whole process of its meaning. It goes far toward putting us to permanent intellectual confusion, and I do not see that any one has as yet alleged, or is ever likely to allege, a sufficient reason for our accepting so dire an alternative. For my own part, therefore, I believe in the immortality of the soul . . . as a supreme act of faith in the reasonableness of God's work." [82]

Thus is the immortal hope the logic of the cosmic process. Our faith in the survival of man's soul fits the universe in the sense that it saves it from irrationality. Evolution, as the method of life upon this planet, is not a madness inconsistent with its own system of harmonious order, but a motive, or purpose, directed to an end. The immortal soul—this is the goal of evolu-

tion. The imperishable spirit, sprung
by some miracle of transmutation from
the flesh, as the organic has sprung
from the inorganic and the animate
from the inanimate—this is the answer to the cosmic riddle. The more
thoroughly the evolutionary process is
understood, the more certain it becomes that the universe has been labor-
ing to the production of a reality that
will survive and fulfil itself. Or, to pass
from scientific to philosophical terms,
that the universe is spirit, and man the
earthly counterpart of the Eternal
which is God! [33]

# VI

SUCH ARE the modern arguments for immortality as applied to man, and to the universe of which man is so distinct a part. It is a temptation to claim these arguments as constituting a proof of immortality, for it is just such arguments that are used to demonstrate truth in many fields. In all that is fundamental in realms available to science, when you come to think of it, there is an almost complete absence of direct observation, or ultimate verification. What we know, or think we know to-day, is based upon a process of reasoning which is conceptive rather than perceptive in character. Confronted by an array of phenomena which demand precise interpretation, science resorts to the device of hypothesis, or inference. We assume a thing to be true which is necessary if facts are to be reduced to order or which permits factual prediction. This is the Baconian method of induction, which is accepted today as furnishing a type of demonstration as persuasive, if not as conclusive, as that of the classical mathematics. In social life as well as in scientific research, it is daily practiced.

Here in a court of law, for example, is a defendant accused of murder. There is no direct evidence of his guilt —nobody saw him kill his alleged victim! But there is a mass of attendant circumstances which can be explained, in detail and altogether, only on the supposition that the defendant committed the crime as charged. And judge and jury do not hesitate to accept the supposition, and to act upon it by convicting and sentencing the offender.

Here in a hospital is a patient who seems to be ill of cancer. Nobody really knows, since nobody has seen the hidden growth. On the other hand there are symptoms which seem to point to this inescapable hypothesis. This man's condition can be explained only on this assumption. By a purely inductive process of reasoning, the physicians come to their conclusion, and prove their faith by laying the patient on the operating table.

Years ago, the famous Professor William Ramsay, in an address before the chemical section of the British Association for the Advancement of Science, described the peculiar qualities of a certain gas. Of these the most remarkable was the fact that it had not yet been discovered—i.e., isolated, observed, and tested. What Professor Ramsay meant was that this new gas was an hypothesis which had become necessary to the understanding of an array of phenomena which had itself

55

been verified. The existence of certain conditions already established in the world of matter made inevitable, as an explanation of these conditions, the parallel existence of certain other conditions which coalesced into the properties of a gas not yet discovered, and thus in actual experience unknown. As little as Darwin hesitated to announce the hypothesis of evolution as an inference from the body of biological facts which he had gathered through twenty years of patient labor, did Professor Ramsay, or any of his colleagues, hesitate to announce, and even describe, this supposititious gas.

Professor Ramsay's discovery is a single episode in the marvelous story of the extension of chemical knowledge in modern times. As recently as my high school days, it was believed that all matter must be ultimately resolved into some seventy-odd elements, which could be seen and studied. In more recent years, it was found that further analysis of matter was necessary—that the so-called basic elements, in other words, were themselves resolvable into other particles still more basic. Thus, subsidiary to atoms, were minute realities which defied the reach and range of microscopic vision. But these were declared to exist on the inferential ground that, if they did not exist, certain facts, constantly under observation, were otherwise inexplicable. That which lay beyond the range of sensory impression, in other words, was still demonstrated to be real by a process of inductive argument from the visible to the invisible, from the known to the unknown. Later experimentation directly verified this indirect method of proof.

And what about the uniformity of nature? No one has seen and tested this alleged uniformity except in part, and that part the tiniest fragment of time and space. The recorded experience of man in nature covers but a tick or two upon the clock face of eternity. Of the future there is no guarantee except in a past of which we know comparatively little. Yet man declares with confidence the uniformity of nature, for the reason that, in the light of such experience as he has, no other conception is consistent with his integrity of thought. The universe and man's life therein are simply not understandable except on the assumption of natural law—and straightway man makes this law of cause and effect a part of the accepted body of human knowledge.

The application of all this to the problem of immortality must be obvious. If there be a future life, it has not been explored, or even visited. Not

yet have such reports as those of
Emanuel Swedenborg, for example,
been received into the records of science
as valid data of experience. In the
same way there has been no return by,
or report from, the dead. The abundant
material of psychological research, as
we have seen, has not been proved in-
dubitably to originate upon the other
side of the grave. But what cannot be
seen beyond may be discovered here.
What death still hides, life may itself
reveal. Man, and the qualities of his
personality; the universe, and its
course of evolution; the spirit, and its
eternal implications—these are facts
which have meaning. The meaning demands explanation. The explanation
demands an hypothesis. And what can
this be but immortality? As applicable
to this vast problem of the soul as to
the routine problems of natural science
and daily experience is the statement

of Professor R. K. Duncan, distinguished chemist:

"If we have a beautiful building of systematized perceptions and conceptions all dove-tailing into one another in the complete expression of an idea, we say that the idea is true, even though it passes all demonstration in experience, because we see in it a perfect harmony, and this harmony pleases us and gives us a feeling of the recognition of truth. . . . It is an act of pure faith. . . . But it is [the faith which is] bred in the very bone of science." [34]

Thus does faith take on the aspect of proof through the processes of reason. To those who accept the processes of reason, it must remain proof. These will ask no further or surer demonstration. Immortality, like natural law, will be to them a part of knowledge.

Yet it still is in essence faith. For reason is itself "an act of pure faith."

Which means that we return at the end
to what we affirmed in the beginning,
that immortality is a necessary part of
that spiritual approach to life which we
accept because it brings to us a harmony of experience which "gives us a
feeling of the recognition of truth"!
The affirmation of it all is rooted in the
inner life. The soul bearing witness to
its own eternal destiny! Mr. Howard
Spring, the English novelist, sums it all
up in a statement as old as Plato, and
as new as his recently published book,
*And Another Thing,* in which it ap-
pears:

"I stand upon the brink of the unknown, utter and unplumbed. I have
never seen as much as a ghost, nor met
any one whose adventures in that direction have satisfied me of validity.
All I can say of a surety is that I believe in the perpetual existence of the
spiritual life. If we accept, as we must,

the theory of the indestructibility of matter, no less must we accept the indestructibility of the spirit with which matter is informed. Having known something of the brightness with which that spirit may burn within its corporeal envelope, I cannot believe that it is lost and utterly cast away." [35]

# VIII

IT IS curious how convincing this faith in immortality becomes when translated from the language of metaphysics into that of common speech. The casual dichotomy of flesh and spirit seems suddenly to take on the aspect of fundamental reality. The survival of personality after death becomes inevitable.

To illustrate what I mean, and to bring this "great argument" to a close on the level not of abstract speculation but of concrete, every-day experience, I append herewith a letter which I addressed to the Editor of the New York *Times* on October 13, 1944.[36] The letter reads as follows:

TO THE EDITOR OF THE NEW YORK TIMES:
I hope that I may not be misunderstood if I protest at a usage of words in the description

of death and burial which seems to be growing upon our newspaper reporters these days. It is difficult to state what I have in mind, but I can illustrate it in the conspicuous case of Wendell Willkie, whose recent death was so sympathetically and reverently handled by the daily press.

The accounts of this tragic episode all began by stating that Mr. Willkie had died at a certain hour and under certain circumstances. Then appeared a succession of statements, of which the following are typical examples:

"Mr. Willkie will be taken to the church this noon from the undertaking establishment . . ."

"Following the service, Mr. Willkie will be taken to the Pennsylvania station . . ."

"Mr. Willkie will be placed in a crypt . . ."

"The throngs walked down the aisle to the pulpit where Mr. Willkie lay in state . . ."

"Mr. Willkie was in an open bronze coffin . . ."

64

# The Affirmation of Immortality

"Wendell L. Willkie sped west last night toward his final resting place."

May I respectfully contend that Mr. Willkie played no such part as described in these quotations taken from several newspapers. Mr. Willkie was not taken to the church from the undertaking establishment, nor to the Pennsylvania station after the service, nor was he "placed in a crypt." Mr. Willkie did not lie in state, nor rest "in an open bronze coffin," nor did he speed west "toward his final resting place." It was Mr. Willkie's body that did these things.

When this great American died, he had "finished his course." All that made him the strong, heroic, lovable man he was, passed away from this earthly scene when he drew his last breath. There was left here only the body—the tenement of clay in which he had lived, the garment of flesh which he had worn. This body was laid away with every token of admiration and affection because it was the sign and symbol of the man. But the man, the personality, the soul—this was gone. Not extinguished, not dead at all—but, as the poet says, "but gone before" to the eternal realm where in due course we shall all be gathered. To speak of Wendell Willkie as himself this body, which must in due course crumble to dust and disappear, involves a kind of sacrilege which offends every higher instinct of the spirit.

This apparently trivial matter of newspaper style and usage is, in its ultimate implications, momentous. It opens up vast metaphysical questions of personal reality, and touches the whole substance of religious faith. To him who believes in immortality and is convinced that, while we *have* a body, we are a *soul*, there can be no compromise on this issue. It is the body that is laved, and laid in state, and borne to the grave, and at last buried. The man lives on untouched, unharmed, unended.

I think of that last dialogue of Socrates, as recorded by Plato in the closing passage of the *Phaedo:*

" 'In what way shall we bury you?' said Crito.

" 'However you wish,' [Socrates] replied, 'only you must catch me first and see that I don't slip away.'

"And then smiling quietly and turning to us, he said:

66

" 'Why, my friends, I can't convince Crito that I am this Socrates, the one who talks with you and argues at length. He thinks that I am that other whom presently he shall see lying dead, and so he asks how he shall bury me. All the words I have spoken to show that when I drink the poison I shall no longer remain with you, but shall go away to some blessed region of the happy dead, are thrown away on him. . . . I would have Crito . . . not say at the funeral that he is laying out Socrates, or carrying Socrates to the grave, or burying him. For you must know, my dearest Crito, that wrong words are not only a fault in themselves, but insinuate evil into the soul. Be brave, therefore, and say you are burying my body. . . .'

"And the man handed the cup to Socrates, who received it cheerfully, . . . and asked, 'What say you? Is it permitted to make a libation to the gods from this cup?'

" 'We prepare only what we think a sufficient draught, Socrates,' he answered.

" 'I understand; but at least we are permitted, nay, obliged to pray the gods to grant us a happy journey from this world to the other. So I pray, and so may it be.' "

# NOTES

This Lecture is an old picture set in a new frame. I have used it as an opportunity to restate ideas already set forth in my *Is Death The End?* (1915), in chapter XII of *Rethinking Religion* (1938), and in many published sermons. The Lecture may be regarded as a kind of summary, in some passages a repetition, of what I have been preaching and writing for more than forty years. I am ready to submit it as my last testament on the subject of immortality.

What is new in this Lecture, at least to me, is the attempt to make plain the essentially spiritual character of the idea of survival after death. All too often this question is discussed apart by itself, as a peculiarly baffling mystery, to be solved, if at all, by strange phenomena of revelation. The alleged resurrection of Jesus is an illustration at one end of the scale, and so-called psychical manifestations an illustration at the other. But immortality is no such mystery! It is rather a normal and natural part of a whole philosophy of life. It belongs with

God, the soul, and the moral law, as an aspect of the spiritual ideal. If this universe is purely materialistic in character, and operated by purely mechanistic laws, then is it as foolish to believe in immortality as to worship God. But if this universe is spirit, then do all postulates of the spirit become instantly true. Immortality is then as inevitable as the destiny of being, as God is inevitable as its source.

The problem, therefore, that confronts us is not immortality, is it true or false? It is rather the all-encompassing problem of our concept of reality. If this concept is spiritual and thus basically religious, then our doubts are over. "O death, where is thy sting? O grave, where is thy victory?"

[1] Quoted in René Fülöp-Miller's *The Saints That Moved the World*, page 131. I have not found this statement in Augustine's works, but Fülöp-Miller is trustworthy. Furthermore, the statement fits the man and the age.

[2] Familiar lines from the *Rubaiyat* of Omar Khayyam, as translated by Edward Fitzgerald.

[3] Spencer's *Autobiography*, Volume II, page 549.

[4] From a letter contributed to Will Durant's

symposium volume, *On the Meaning of Life*, pages 30–35. The letter is quoted in full in M. Lincoln Schuster's *A Treasury of the World's Great Letters*, pages 507–510. Dr. Durant calls this "a delightful piece." Mr. Schuster is content to refer to it as "characteristic." I find it more characteristic than delightful. It is a document more typical of 1932, when written, than it is of this sadder and wiser day.

In reference to Mr. Mencken's statement that the belief in immortality issues from "the puerile egos of inferior men," it may be well to list the names of a few of the "inferior men." In ancient times, Socrates, Plato, Cicero, Seneca; in more modern times, Descartes, Spinoza, Kant, Goethe, Fiske, Eddington, and Lodge. If immortality is a delusion, says Martineau, in his *Endeavors After the Christian Life* (page 117), "we know who are those who are mistaken. Not the mean and groveling souls . . . the deceived are the great and holy. . . . Whom are we to reverence, and what can we believe, if the inspirations of the highest natures are but cunningly-devised fables?"

[5] From Paul's great pæan to immortality in his First Epistle to the Corinthians *XV*.

[6] A series of remarkable volumes by Stewart Edward White. *The Betty Book*, published in 1937; followed by *Across the Unknown* (1939) and *The Unobstructed Universe* (1940). In reviewing *The Betty Book*, I spoke of it as "an honest report of firsthand and unquestionably genuine experience . . . embodying a system of spiritual truth as sane as it is sublime."

[7] A scrambled but accurate quotation, page 118. Maeterlinck's book seems largely forgotten—it was published in this country thirty-three years ago! But I know of no more temperate, convincing and beautiful statement of the problem of immortality.

[8] I find this quoted in *A Catholic Looks at His World* (1945), by Francis E. McMahon. The source is not given, but I assume the passage is taken from the famous *Holmes-Pollock Letters*.

[9] Quoted in Albert Lazenby's *Tides of the Spirit* (1905), a volume of selections from the writings of James Martineau. See page 187.

[10] The only time I ever saw and heard John Fiske was on the evening he delivered this Ingersoll Lecture at Sanders Theatre, Cambridge, December 19, 1900. I remember being

greatly impressed, but surprised when the lecturer abruptly stopped, with his argument, I felt, unfinished. Fiske died the following July 4th. The Lecture was published in the autumn of 1901, with the Note that "it is possible that he designed amplifying it."

[11] See Aldous Huxley's *The Perennial Philosophy* (1945), a fascinating anthology of spiritual wisdom.

[12] See Thomas H. Huxley's famous letter to Charles Kingsley, published in his son Leonard's *Life and Letters of Thomas H. Huxley*, Volume I, page 233. This is perhaps the noblest statement ever made of the agnostic attitude toward truth.

[13] See Plato's Dialogue, *Meno*, Section 81 in the Jowett translation.

[14] See *Phaedrus*, Section 245, in the Jowett translation.

[15] See *Canto XLV*.

[16] Quoted in that unique and absorbing anthology, *The Practical Cogitator*, edited by Charles P. Curtis, Jr., and Ferris Greenslet (1945), page 556.

[17] See Chapter II, page 109.

[18] See Matthew Arnold's poem.

[19] See Chapter II, page 9.

[20] See my *Rethinking Religion,* pp. 217–222.

[21] See Volume II, chapter III, page 347.

[22] See *The Life of Alice Freeman Palmer* (1908), page 327.

[23] From a contemporary newspaper review of the first performance of the symphony after the composer's death.

[24] See *Thoughts on Life and Death* (1937), pages 199–200.

[25] Quoted in *The Practical Cogitator* (see above), page 38.

[26] I am glad to quote this passage if only to remind modern readers of the existence of this charming essay which does equal credit to two great and good men. Irving's first impression of the bleak and bare Scotch landscape as later transfigured by the literary associations of the scenes is itself a parable of the spiritual life.

[27] The familiar and ever-glorious passage from Shakespeare's *Hamlet,* Act II, scene II.

[28] See the familiar speech in *The Tempest,* Act IV, scene I.

[29] See *Macbeth,* Act V, scene V.

[30] From one of the most memorable of Robert Frost's poems, "Fire and Ice," published in his volume *New Hampshire* (1923).

[31] See Francis Darwin's *Life and Letters of Charles Darwin* (1904), Volume I, page 282.

[32] See *The Destiny of Man*, pages 115–116.

[33] See my *Is Death The End?*, Chapter VI.

[34] See *The New Knowledge* (1905), page 255. The concluding chapter of this book, "The Validity of the New Knowledge," is all much to the point.

[35] See page 244. This entire book is to be commended as a convincing and strangely beautiful account of the recovery, or rather discovery, of religion by a sensitive and highly cultivated mind under the impact of the tragic events of our time.

[36] This letter was not published. But it drew a personal letter from the editor of the *Times* in which he wrote: "Thanks so much for your criticism of the Willkie stories. It is very interesting and instructive, and of course you are right."

The *Phaedo* passage is taken from "The Judgment of Socrates," a translation by Paul Elmer More in the Riverside Literature Series, Houghton Mifflin & Co., 1898.